An Hour's Walk Round Roman York

After your visit to the Undercroft Museum in York Minster where structural remains of the Headquarters Building of the Fortress and the best finds from the recent excavations are on display, leave by the south door (*1*). Notice the re-erected Roman column opposite (see page 9).

Follow the foot-walk skirting the choir of the Minster and turn right past the half-timbered building, St. William's College in College Street, and then sharp left into Goodramgate. Before you is Monk Bar (*2*). Ascend the wall by the steps to the right of the Bar and walk along the wall for about 40 yards. Below you will be seen the rounded remains of the east corner tower — the Aldwark Tower (*4*) and an interval tower (*3*). At the corner the fortress wall stands to its full height, excluding parapet, of 16 ft. The medieval hall beyond is that of the Merchant Taylors.

Return to Monk Bar, descend to ground level, cross the street and climb on to the City walls by means of the narrow flight of steps in Monk Bar. As you proceed towards Bootham Bar you are walking on the thirteenth century wall built on top of a series of earlier mounds which overlie the Roman fortress wall. Pause when you reach a bronze plaque of 1898 recording the gift of this part of the walls back to the city by Edwin Gray. You are now near the site of one of the four gates into the fortress—the *porta decumana* (*5*). Looking into the city you will see a narrow cobbled street, Chapter House Street which overlies the Roman *via decumana* (*6*).

Continue along the city walls past the attractive gardens of Gray's Court and the Deanery. The walls eventually take a turn of 90 degrees to the left: this is because they are following the precise line of the Roman fortress. This angle marks the site of the north corner of the fortress. From this vantage point look back along the medieval moat outside the walls which lies further out than the earlier Roman ditches. The view inside this stretch of wall is the finest in York; The Minster (*1*) (built over the Principia—headquarters' building of the fortress), the Chapter House and the Minster Library. Continue to Bootham Bar (*7*) which overlies another gateway in the fortress—the *porta principalis dextra*—part of which is preserved in a modern underground building adjoining the Bar. Through the window to the left inside the Bar you look down on High Petergate (*8*)—part of the *via principalis* of the fortress.

Descend from the walls at Bootham Bar: cross the busy street below you (St. Leonard's) where you will see another small section of the fortress wall (*9*). A plaque records that it was built under the direction of the Emperor Constantius Chlorus c. A.D. 300.

Walk towards the City Art Gallery with the statue of William Etty in the square in front of it, and very shortly turn left down a lane marked 'University of York staff car park'. The medieval King's Manor is on your right. Pass through the gate into the Museum Gardens where you will see to the left the outside of the Multangular Tower (*10*), the west corner of the Roman fortress. Adjoining this tower is a 40-yard sector of the fourth century fortress wall with vestiges of another interval tower. This wall, 17 ft high, stands to its full height (only the parapet is missing) and with the Multangular Tower ranks as one of the finest surviving pieces of Roman masonry in Britain.

The Roman wall butts onto a Norman archway which constituted the entrance to the medieval Hospital of St. Leonard's (*11*), situated close to the main gates of the Museum Gardens. In this archway are Roman coffins and other archaeological objects including the dismantled stones from a Roman stone-lined cistern. It was found in Bishophill in 1872 and is one of many which must have existed at street junctions in the Colonia or civil town. The inlet and outlet channels show that it was fed by a constant flowing stream of water.

Return to the Multangular Tower and following the sign 'Anglian Tower' pass through the medieval wall by a little door into the garden of the Public Library. This has been attractively laid out to display the inside of the Multangular Tower, the fourth-century fortress wall on either side of it, a unique Anglian tower let into the Roman wall, and subsequent Danish, Norman and Plantagenet defences. The coffins on the lawn and within the Multangular Tower are Roman. The arcading on top of the tower is medieval.

Re-entering the Museum Gardens visit the new Roman Exhibition in the Yorkshire Museum (*13*) an attractive and modern display of some of the best items from ~~one of the f~~~~~~ of Roman remains to be found anywhere in Britain.

The Multangular Tower is diagonally opposite the Aldwark Tower so that you have now walked exactly half way round the fortress.

Should you wish to extend your tour to cover the whole of the fortress the places to visit are: St. Helen's Square (21), site of the south-west gate, with a plaque on the wall of the Yorkshire Insurance Building; Feasegate, site of the south corner tower under street and shops opposite an entrance to British Home Stores on the left side of which an inscription records the line of the Roman wall; St. Sampson's Square, where the 'Roman Bath' (15) is an inn named from the remains of the legionary bath-house to be seen within (see page 10); King's Square, named from the Viking kings who once dwelt in the remains of the Roman south-east gatehouse, with two plaques on the front of one of the shops of which the more detailed and informative is also the nearer to its site. Prior application must be made to the York Archaeological Trust to view the Roman sewer (see page 28) and to the college of Ripon and York St. John to view a small but interesting collection of Roman finds in Gray's Court (22), next door to the Treasurer's House (14) where there is a column base and cobbled street visible in a cellar. The interval tower in Lendal (23) is now reburied.

Across the river a pleasant walk along the city wall from Lendal Bridge (16) to the Norman castle mound of Baile Hill (19) will encompass the site of the Roman town. But only opposite the railway station does the city wall overlie the Roman town wall, and part at least of the castle site, as burials show, lay outside the town. The Roman road passed at or near Micklegate Bar (17), where you may leave the wall (20) to visit the vaulted tomb (see page 23) if you have permission. From Victoria Bar (18) Victor Street leads to Carr Lane where a sharp drop in the medieval stonework at the base of the brick wall on your left indicates the Roman terrace (see page 17). It is a short walk from Carr Lane to Micklegate where inside the church of St. Martin-cum-Gregory is a fine Roman tomb relief.

CONTENTS

Acknowledgements

Photographs appearing on pages 9, 10, 11, 14, 16, 17, 18, 19, 22, 23, 25, 26 and 27 are published with permission of the Royal Commission on Historical Monuments (England) Crown Copyright.

The photograph appearing on page 8 is published with permission of the Yorkshire Museum, York. The photograph on page 28 is published by permission of the York Archaeological Trust.

Other photographs have been provided through the courtesy of the late Mr. L. P. Wenham.

The Status of Roman York

ROMAN YORK, named Eburacum or Eboracum, had a distinguished history. It began in A.D. 71 as the military base of the Ninth Legion in its campaigns against the Brigantes and remained as the headquarters for the powerful Roman army in north Britain for more than 300 years.

In an empire based on military might the strength of this army gave to York considerable importance, greater indeed than that of the other two permanent legionary fortresses in Britain, at Chester and at Caerleon, in Gwent. It was visited by the military leaders of Rome including the emperors themselves. Two emperors died in Britain, both in Eburacum: Septimius Severus in A.D. 211, and Constantius I (called Chlorus) in A.D. 306. Upon the latter's death his son Constantine was proclaimed his successor by the legionaries here in York who thus started him on his road to the emperorship. We know him as Constantine the Great. In the Yorkshire Museum there is a splendid stone head representing him as a young man, a fitting memorial to this event in York's history which had greatest world importance.

Clearly Eburacum must have had accommodation and amenities fit for emperors and indeed for empress and court as well, because for the three years A.D. 208 to 211, Severus whilst directing campaigns in north Britain governed the Roman empire from Eburacum until his death.

Historians speak of a palace in Eburacum, and a great city grew up beside the fortress, holding as an honour the highest possible status, that of a *colonia*, which gave it self-government. In the third century York was the capital of Lower Britain, one of the two provinces into which Britain was then divided (the other capital probably being London), and York remained a provincial capital in the fourth century when Britain was administered as a group of four provinces in the prefecture of the Gauls.

In A.D. 314 three British bishops, those of York, London and either Lincoln or Colchester attended the Christian council at Arles. In those days church organisation closely reflected provincial administration. There were likely to have been many more than three bishops in Britain, and therefore it is possible that these three were the metropolitans from three of the four provincial capitals.

The new architectural splendour given to the fortress at Eburacum about A.D. 300 provided a dramatic setting for the military headquarters of Constantius I at the time of his death in the city in A.D. 306. Brash and theatrical it might well have seemed to a visitor more used to the older glories of the central area of the Roman empire, but to king Crocus, a German from outside the empire transported to Britain with his tribesmen for military service with Constantius, it would no doubt have seemed grand and metropolitan.

The memorials that time has left us are not just those of dignity and splendour. York was a busy cosmopolitan town, largely concerned with the army but also engaged in commerce on its own account. In addition to a palace and luxurious houses there were poorer homes and humble workshops as well. It was a place where many people died at a much earlier age than they do to-day but also a community where a close and happy family life was possible and where a slave could rise to become his master's heir.

Chronological Table

B.C.   BRITAIN   55   First Roman invasion of Southern Britain by Julius Caesar

A.D. ROME		A.D. BRITAIN		A.D. YORK	
41-54	Emperor Claudius	43	Conquest of Britain began: four legions including IX Hispana		
54-68	Emperor Nero	c. 47	Brigantes under Cartimandua allied with Rome		
69	'Year of the Four Emperors'. Civil War	69	Brigantes broke with Rome		
69-79	Emperor Vespasian	71-4	Brigantes conquered	71	First wooden fortress: Headquarters of Legio IX Hispana
		79-84	Campaigns of Agricola in N. Britain and Caledonia	c. 81	Second wooden fortress

Emperor Vespasian

Emperor Trajan

Emperor Hadrian

A.D. ROME		A.D. BRITAIN		A.D. YORK	
98-117	Emperor Trajan			107-8	Fortress rebuilt in stone
117-138	Emperor Hadrian	122-38	Hadrian's Wall built	c. 122	Legio VI Victrix replaced Legio IX
193-211	Emperor Septimius Severus	c. 197	Period of disorder in North Britain, followed by building activity on Hadrian's Wall and its hinterland	c. 200	Fortress defences and town rebuilt
		208-11	Severus in Britain, War and Victory	208-11	Severus and the Imperial Court made York their base.
211-217	Emperor Marcus Antoninus (Caracalla)			211	Severus died and cremated in York
				c. 213	Eburacum made capital of Britannia Inferior. Town given status of Colonia

Emperor Septimius Severus

Emperor Marcus Antoninus (Caracalla)

A.D. ROME	A.D. BRITAIN	A.D. YORK
284-305 Emperor Diocletian introduced system of two Augusti and two Caesars	286-296 First Carausius and then Allectus declared themselves Emperors of Britain	c. 300 Fortress defences partially rebuilt in grander style
293-306 Constantius I (Chlorus) Caesar of the West	c. 300 Hadrian's Wall (decayed and neglected in later third century) repaired and strengthened	c. 300 New Military command, Dux Britanniarum in charge of field army. H.Q. at York
306-337 Emperor Constantine (the Great)		306 Constantius died in York. Constantine proclaimed his successor there
		314 Bishop of Eburacum attended Council of Arles

Emperor
Constantius I
(Chlorus)

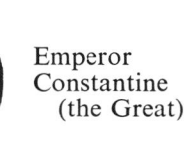

Emperor
Constantine
(the Great)

A.D. ROME	A.D. BRITAIN	A.D. YORK
367-383 Emperor Gratian	367 Confederacy of barbarians ravaged N. Britain. Hadrian's Wall outflanked Fullofaudes, Duke of Britain, routed	
	369 Count Theodosius repairs and strengthens Hadrian's Wall	
395-423 Emperor Honorius		
406 Rome plundered by Goths under Alaric	407-11 Constantine III, usurper emperor from Britain, occupies Gaul with most of the British garrison	c. 400 Germanic levies at York
	410 Honorius instructed the Britons to look to their own defence and Hadrian's Wall abandoned	after c. 450 Parts of the town are deserted and the Roman Ouse bridge destroyed and the road approaching from the S.W. overlaid by ploughsoil

Eburacon to York

York sounds very different from *Eburacon*, but philologists can trace the modern name back through its various stages to its Celtic origins. The Britons first named the place, *Eburacon*, meaning in their language either 'the place where the yew trees grow', or 'the place belonging to Eburos'. The Romans latinised the ending and called it *Eburacum*, or altered it to *Eboracum*. They also used a boar as a badge for the town. The Anglo-Saxons used their own word for boar and their own word for town, and called it *Evorwic*. The Vikings pronounced this badly and wrote it, *Jorvik*, from which comes the modern York.

Bronze Mouse.
Found in the grounds of The Mount School, Dalton Terrace: probably originally with a burial.

The Brigantes

York was one of the nine places listed in the Geography of Ptolemy, written about A.D. 140, as in the territory of the Brigantes. We do not know the exact boundaries but on the basis of these nine places their territory must have included the ancient counties of Lancashire, the North and West Ridings of Yorkshire, Cumberland, Westmorland and Durham. East of York another people, the Parisi, occupied a territory extending from the Humber into the limestone hills north of Pickering, defined in the archaeological record as the Arras culture, of which typical remains are the square-ditched barrows easily recognisable on air photographs.

Two of the Brigantian places mentioned by Ptolemy, *Camulodunum* and *Rigodunum* were originally the names of pre-Roman hill-forts at Almondbury and Ingleborough, whilst there was another large hill-fort at Barwick-in-Elmet, and at Stanwick near Richmond there was an important fortified royal centre or *oppidum*. The Brigantes occupied a large, often mountainous area, with many different types of terrain and natural sub-divisions, and before the Roman conquest were a confederacy rather than one united tribe, with rival noble families and local chiefs, difficult to control and prone to power struggles.

Little is known of York itself before the Romans beyond the name, a group of burials in a native tradition, a late iron age belt-plate, and the indication of a cross-ridge dyke. There may never have been more than a small farm on the south-west side of the Ouse where there was the largest area of well-drained land suitable for farming, but a site at a river crossing (and where the Brigantes held land formerly occupied by the Parisi as the presence of square-ditched barrows within four miles to south and east shows) is suitable for a stronghold.

The Roman Conquest

The Romans first raided Britain in 55 B.C., but it was not until A.D. 43 that they came to conquer. By A.D. 47 they held all of England south of a line from the Humber to the Severn. At first their main pressure was in the centre to the north-west and by A.D. 60 they had established a legion at Wroxeter near Shrewsbury, and by the late sixties also at Gloucester.

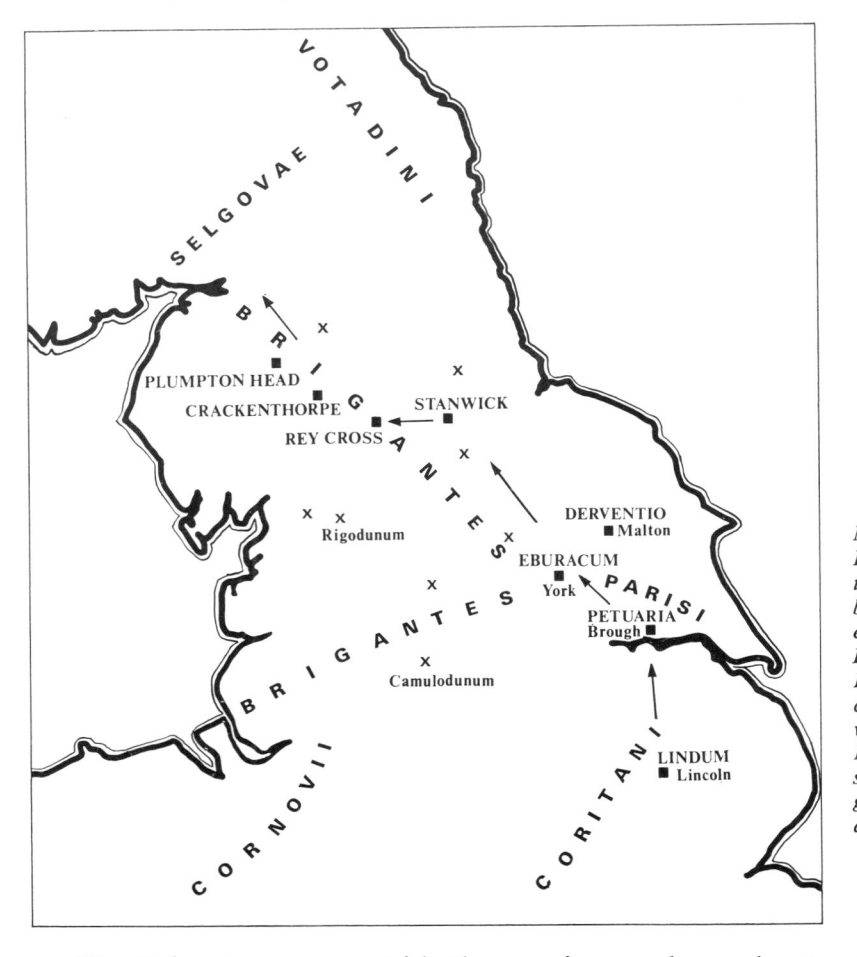

N. Britain in A.D. 71. It is impossible to define the territory of the Brigantes by exact boundaries. The eight places mentioned by Ptolemy in addition to Eburacum are marked by crosses. Places associated with the advance of the Ninth legion are marked by squares. Arrows mark general direction of the advance.

The Brigantes were outside the province and were kept quiet on the northern flank by an alliance with their queen Cartimandua and by Roman money. Refugee craftsmen moving north from the conquered territory produced fine art metalwork, a late flowering of native culture among the Brigantes that implies a basis of wealth in their nobility best attributed to Roman subsidy. Two examples in the Yorkshire Museum are the well-known terret (harness ring) in the shape of a horned head from Aldborough and a fine enamelled belt-plate from York itself.

For the story of the Roman conquest of the Brigantes we are dependent on a now incomplete and sometimes biased account by the historian Tacitus and various not very explicit references by other authors. It is clear that Cartimandua was not entirely secure in her position as ruler of the Brigantes, and the Romans had already had to intervene at least three times to maintain her authority. Her main rival was her husband Venutius and Tacitus represents the strife as between a slighted husband and adulterous queen, but it is best seen as a political struggle between rival chieftains.

Venutius was a powerful personality and an ambitious man. In A.D. 69-70 civil strife in the empire and divided loyalties in the British legions enabled him to seize power without fear of Roman intervention, and to drive Cartimandua into exile. The fortifications at Stanwick near Richmond used to be closely associated with Venutius as a last minute reaction to the Roman presence. Recent excavation and analysis suggest an important royal centre or *oppidum* with a longer history, carefully and strategically sited with vast strongly defended enclosures, containing a large settlement and designed to administer and control a large area.

The Multangular Tower, the west corner tower of the legionary fortress, built in the fourth century.

Once the new Roman emperor Vespasian was fully established and revolts in Judaea and Holland quelled, he appointed a new governor, Q. Petillius Cerialis, who set sail for Britain in the spring of A.D. 71, bringing with him a replacement legion, the Second Adiutrix from Nijmegen in Holland. This he placed in the fortress at Lincoln, vacated by the Ninth which he moved up to a new base, York, in Brigantian territory.

The main direction of the campaign is fixed by the relative positions of Lincoln, York and Stanwick. A fort at Brough commanded the crossing of the Humber; others at Malton and Hayton guarded the flank against attack from the Parisi of East Yorkshire; and legionary camps, each a day's march apart at Rey Cross, Crackenthorpe, and Plumpton Head show the line of advance beyond Stanwick over Stainmore into Cumberland. York provided a firm base for the northern advance, held any threat from the Pennine Dales, and had good communications to the rear and with the western legion.

The Legionary Fortress

The site is typical of a legionary fortress, on a ridge of higher ground within the junction of a tidal river (the Ouse) and a tributary which could provide a harbour (the Foss). In plan the fortress was a rectangle with rounded corners with long axis orientated north-east to south-west and covered 50 acres.

The main gate, *porta praetoria*, was central to the south-west side which faced the Ouse and a bridge. The site of this gate is now in St. Helen's Square. Stonegate, the street leading from this square to the Minster, is mostly on the line of the Roman *via praetoria*. Petergate is mostly on the line of the Roman *via principalis*, which linked the gates on the north-west and south-east sides, the *portae principales*, on the sites of Bootham Bar and King's Square. A rear gate, the *porta decumana*, central on the north-east side, lies hidden under the medieval rampart.

Stone column 22 ft. long and 3 ft. in diameter, found under the Minster in 1969.
It was part of an arcade in the great hall of the headquarters building. It has been
re-erected in a new position nearly opposite the south door of the Minster.

The central position in the fortress is now occupied by the Minster which lies on its own liturgical east to west axis diagonal to that of the Roman fortress, and indeed the modern town. In Roman times this position was occupied by the *principia* or headquarters building which in its own way was as dominating and imposing a building as the Minster. At the rear of a court-yard stood a great hall which at one period of its history was larger than the Minster nave. The north-west end was below the central tower and it extended diagonally across the South Transept so that excavations to strengthen the Minster foundations have revealed a considerable part of it which is now open to visitors in the Undercroft Museum.

One of the great columns lay full length as it had collapsed long after the Romans had left. Panels of painted plaster fallen from the walls have been reconstructed and are in the museum. The splendid stone head of Constantine the Great, twice life size, from an official statue which perhaps once graced the headquarters building, was found in Stonegate before 1823, and is now in the Yorkshire Museum (*see page* 27).

Bath House in St. Sampson's Square: the apse of the caldarium or hot room. The pilae or pillars in the centre supported the floor.

Other buildings in the fortress included the commandant's house, officers' quarters, barrack blocks, hospital, stores and baths, but apart from scattered fragments we only know the details of a few barracks, part of a tribune's house and a late bath building. The baths, on the Turkish-bath principle, were an essential feature of Roman life, and in the fourth century the York soldiers had their bath-house inside the fortress. Parts of the hot room with under-floor heating ducts, and a cold plunge bath are preserved under 'The Roman Bath' Inn in St. Sampson's Square.

The history of the fortress is known from excavations on the defences. These consisted at all periods of an earth rampart and ditches, but the rampart, at first faced with turf work and surmounted by a timber palisade, was after the early second century subsidiary to a stone wall.

History of the Fortress Defences

(1) A.D. 71. The ramparts of the first fortress were rapidly constructed with the materials readily available; green boughs were lopped and trimmed and laid as a foundation, onto which earth dug out of a surrounding ditch was built into a bank and faced with turves.

Model of the timber tower of the legionary fortress. Second, Agricolan, phase, dating c. A.D. 80. Based on discoveries in Davygate in 1955.

(2) about A.D. 80. During Agricola's governorship a more permanent character was given to the defences. A foundation of heavy beams of seasoned wood was laid over the spread remains of the first rampart. A new earth bank was erected on this, revetted with turf-work, surmounted by a palisade, strengthened with heavily timbered towers, and surrounded by a double ditch. The buildings inside the fortress were timber-framed with wattle and daub infill. Great cooking ovens at the back of the rampart (the base of one can be seen near the Multangular Tower) were kept away from the buildings to prevent fire.

Commemorative tablet found 1854 in King's Square. It records the building of the stone gateway there under the Emperor Trajan c. A.D. 107-8, by 'Leg VIIII', i.e., by Legio IX.

(3) A.D. 107-8.   This date is provided by an inscription now in the York-shire Museum which implies that the south-east gate (King's Square) was then being rebuilt in stone. Evidence from elsewhere in the fortress demonstrates that the inner ditch was then filled in with the previous turf facing which was replaced by a stone wall, with stone towers.

(4) Late second or early third century.   The whole of the defences were rebuilt on securer foundations. To this date belong the surviving remains at the east corner. The fortress wall emerges from below the medieval wall at a height of 16 ft. and then reduces to its footings. The wall is 6 ft. wide at

Conjectural view of East Corner Tower in Roman times.

STEWART LACK

base narrowing to 5 ft. at the top. It is made of grouted rubble, faced inside and out with small dressed blocks of white Tadcaster stone. A cobbled walk ran behind the wall on top of the earth bank and at a lower level than the wall top. The ruins of two internal towers can be seen adjoining the wall.

(5) About A.D. 300.   The defences were again rebuilt except for the section from the south-east to the north-east gates which includes the east corner. The new wall was similar to the old except that the facing was bonded to the core by a tile band and had a tile cornice. This can still be seen at the

East corner Aldwark tower of the legionary fortress and adjacent wall near Monk Bar, fourth, Severan, phase, c. A.D. 200.

The small clay mound in the Tower is part of the rampart of the second phase, c. A.D. 80. It is the oldest visible part of Eburacum.

west angle where there is also the stump of a great projecting tower, the Multangular Tower, matched by another (not now visible) at the south angle. Along the south-west side, facing the Ouse, were six only slightly less imposing interval towers and a great gritstone gatehouse.

The reasons for these changes are not always certain. (3) can be regarded as part of a general consolidation applied to all three British legionary fortresses at about this time; that at Caerleon was reconstructed in A.D. 99-100 and Chester soon after A.D. 102. (4) The thoroughgoing nature of the rebuilding suggests that the earlier defences had not been altogether satisfactory and there is some evidence of weak foundations. It is possible that work was done in preparation for or during the visit of the Emperor Severus to York A.D. 210-11. (5) is often said to be rebuilding after a Roman defeat, but the new architectural frontispiece added to the river front of the fortress suggests that it had attained a new dignity, probably that of becoming the seat of the new *Dux Britanniarum*, commander of the land forces of all Britain.

Inside the fortress timber buildings have been found, for example near St. William's College and off Blake Street, which must relate to the timber defences. The headquarters building was first built in stone in the early second century (Trajan-Hadrian), but its next reconstruction in the early fourth century was Constantinian rather than Constantian. The exact date of its collapse formerly thought to be the ninth century, is now disputed.

The Garrison

The legion was a large self-contained corps of more than 5,000 Roman citizens who were professional soldiers. Mainly infantry, the legion also contained a detachment of cavalry and various specialised sections. The commanding officer, *legatus legionis*, was serving a three or four year term as part of a career which involved military and administrative posts throughout the empire and culminated in his becoming a consul. The basic unit of the legion was the century of 80 men, commanded by a centurion and grouped in cohorts.

Tile Stamps of the Ninth and Sixth Legions.

The Ninth *Hispana* or Spanish legion, so called from earlier campaigns, came to Britain from Pannonia in Central Europe in A.D. 43, and was established at Lincoln by A.D. 47. It was engaged in campaigns amongst the Brigantes in A.D. 51-2 while commanded by Caesius Nasica, and was cut up by rebels during the revolt of Boudicca in A.D. 60-1 while commanded by Petillius Cerialis. It was brought to York in A.D. 71 when Cerialis was governor, and our last record of it there is in A.D. 107-8. During Hadrian's reign it was moved to Nijmegen and later to the eastern half of the Roman empire where it suffered some disaster as a result of which it was disbanded before A.D. 165.

Lead Sealing found 1954 in Blossom Street inscribed P(rovinciae) B(ritanniae) I(nferioris). The bull was the badge of the Sixth Legion.

The Sixth *Victrix* or victorious legion came to Britain in A.D. 122 or a little earlier from Xanten on the Rhine having previously been at Neuss also on the Rhine. It was responsible for the building of much of Hadrian's Wall, with its turrets and forts. It remained the garrison at York until the Roman troops were withdrawn but certainly had hard campaigning in Scotland as well as garrison duties. Its badge was a bull which was also adopted as the badge of the province of Lower Britain.

14

EBURACUM (Roman York) on Modern Street Plan

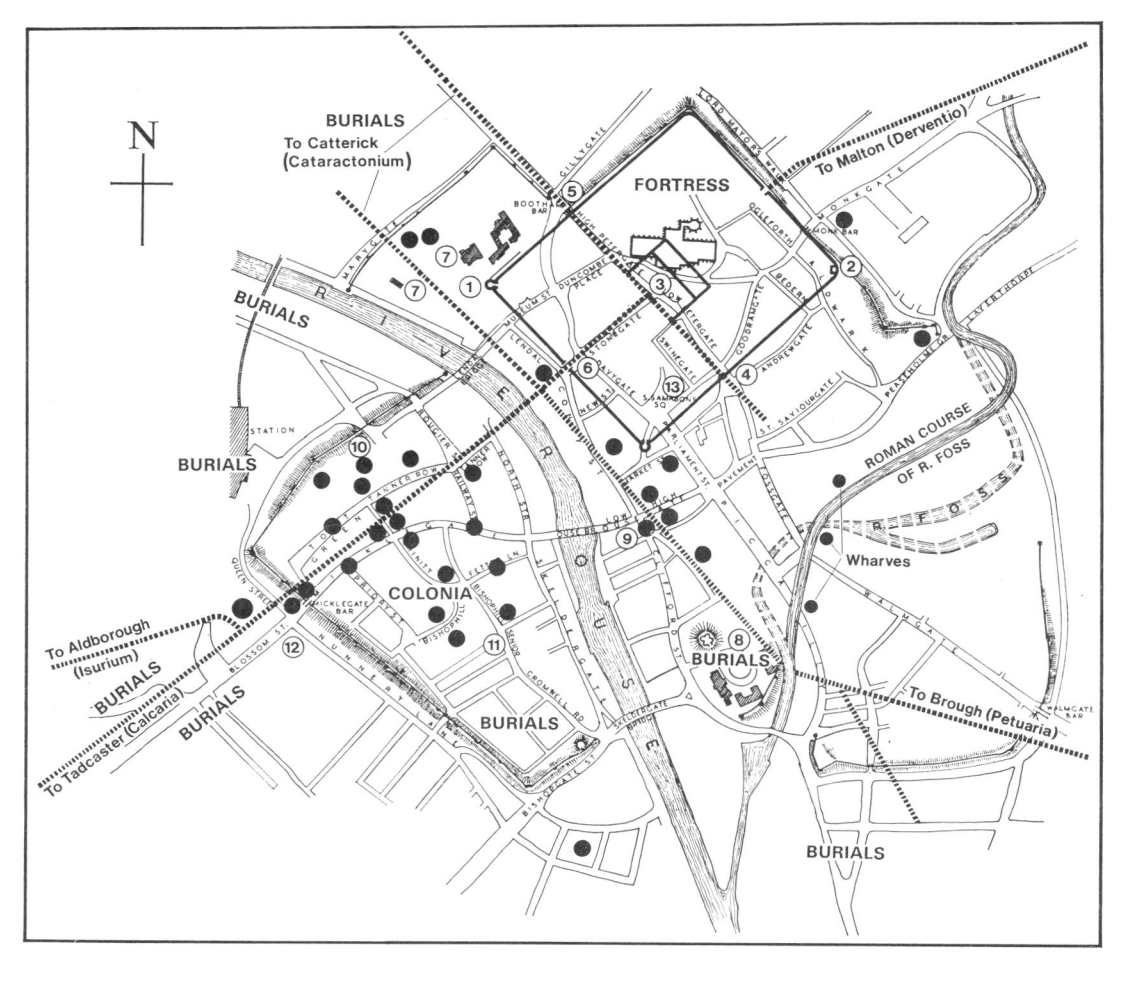

● Sites of Roman Buildings

(1) Multangular Tower
(2) Aldwark Tower
(3) Headquarters Building under Minster
(4) King's Square
(5) Bootham Bar
(6) St. Helen's Square
(7) Yorkshire Museum

(8) Find spot of Julia Victoriana's coffin
(9) Nessgate
(10) Bath House near railway offices.
(11) Bishophill Senior
(12) Find spot of statue of Mars
(13) St. Sampson's Square Bath House

This map does not include features excavated after 1971. The course of the road from Tadcaster to the Roman Ouse Bridge can be disputed.

The Town

Every great military camp attracts civilians to provide for the material, spiritual and cultural needs of the soldiers. Since the whole area of the fortress was required for military purposes, the traders, wives, camp followers and others settled outside and a small township grew up. Such a settlement was known technically as the *canabae* or booths. Where the garrison was permanent it could grow with the course of years into a town of some size, and eventually become a self-governing community, *vicus*, *municipium* or *colonia* according to its importance.

At York the settlement began with timber buildings along some of the roads leading out of the fortress. From the south-west gate a main road crossed the river by bridge and climbed straight up the hill opposite to cross the medieval walls at or near Micklegate Bar. The most favourable site for settlement was along this road and a considerable town developed on the south-west bank of the Ouse which had by A.D. 237 become a *colonia* and may earlier have gained independence from legionary control as a *municipium*. The most likely occasion for the granting of *colonia* status to York was during the residence of the Emperor Severus at York (A.D. 210-11) or when it became the capital of Lower Britain under his successor Caracalla.

Dedication stone to the Egyptian god Serapis found 1770 in Toft Green. 'To the Holy God Serapis, Claudius Hieronymianus, commanding officer of the Legion VI Victrix built this temple from its foundation.'

Although the site of the *colonia* has been identified on the south-west bank of the Ouse, where considerable remains of Roman building have been found from time to time and only there are there sufficient evidences of a town worthy of the status, it should be noted that there was also some civilian settlement on the north-east side of the river, particularly in the Spurriergate-Nessgate area outside the south angle of the fortress where were a bath-building and temples. A replica of a dedication stone from a temple of Hercules has been let into the wall of the Midland Bank in Nessgate where the original was found. Wharves have been found along the Roman course of the river Foss which was probably the main harbour, and a mosaic south of the fortress east angle.

South-west of the Ouse the main public buildings of the *colonia*, such as the *basilica* (a large hall combining the functions of town hall and law court) and the forum or market place, have yet to be discovered together with the great official inscriptions and the major dedications connected with the official worship of the town. A great colonnaded building of majestic proportions stood on the site of George Hudson Street on the hill fronting the entrance to the fortress on the opposite side of the river. An altar with a dedication combining the *genius* of Eboracum with the divinity of the emperor comes from nearby, but the evidence is insufficient to make a confident identification with the *basilica*. But a large building of some architectural stature stood within the angle of Micklegate and Skeldergate on the site of the old Queen's Hotel. The remains standing to some height and including a small window have unfortunately had to be reburied after losing some of the upper courses.

The town developed from buildings strung out along the main road which throughout its history was to serve as its main axis, a road not exactly re-presented by any modern street although it approximates to the line of Toft Green and Tanner Row. Early burials and religious dedications have been found alongside this road as far out as The Mount but some burials are within the later built-up area.

There is not enough evidence to trace the growth of the town in detail but second century timber buildings have been found some way from the main road both to the north-west and south-east. On the north-west they extended up to the medieval rampart; on the south-east a bronze-worker's shop had been established on the site of the now demolished church of St. Mary Bishop-hill Senior. Contemporary burials in the Old Baile near Skeldergate Bridge and under the medieval rampart to the north-west demonstrate that both these sites were at or near the then limits of the town. Along the line of the road there was a timber building as far out as Blossom Street. All the later built-up area is included between these points but the second-century development was sporadic and less dense than later.

At some time a little before or a little after A.D. 200 the bronze workshop at Bishophill was burnt and replaced by two larger stone buildings. The hill slope was levelled and terraced with a stone wall revetting the terrace. This massive terrace was not a local feature but was found in 1973 under the next building block to the north and dated to the third/fourth centuries. It survived into the middle ages and its course can be identified by property boundaries as extending the whole length of the town parallel to the river. Moreover there were probably others above and below it.

Silver ring inscribed 'To the god Sucelus'.
Found 1875 in St. Maurice's Road.

17

Civil engineering works on the scale implied by this terracing suggest official town planning under the authority of any *municipium* or for the foundation of the *colonia* itself. Although first recorded in A.D. 237, the status of *colonia* may well have been granted by the emperor Severus during his residence in York. Particularly to be associated with that emperor's known partiality for the cult of Serapis is the founding at York of a temple to Serapis, erected at the expense of the legionary commander Claudius Hieronymianus, whom we know from the rest of his career to have been resident at York around A.D. 200.

The dedication stone to this temple (*see page* 16) was found in Toft Green not very far from large and imposing third-century bath buildings found in 1839 and 1939 near to and on the site of Hudson House and the old Railway Station. These were probably part of a double suite for males and females, and had a complicated system of drains and water supply. They may well have belonged to another large building known only from literary sources, the *domus palatina* or palace where the emperor Severus resided with his court between A.D. 208 and 211.

The street plan was probably a close grid with some of the house blocks only 120 ft. wide. There was a piped water supply with fountains or cisterns set at intervals along the cobbled streets. We do not know a great deal about the third-century buildings. Apart from the possible public buildings in George Hudson Street, houses had white limestone walls with half-timbered upper storeys and roofs of red tile or sometimes stone.

Statue of the god Mars.
Found on the site of the Bar Convent in
Blossom Street in 1880.

Most of the evidence belongs to the fourth-century town when considerable rebuilding seems to have taken place. Excavations by Wenham, Ramm and more recently by the York Archaeological Trust have revealed houses on Bishophill and at Clementhorpe. A fairly standard house developed, large and luxurious, with under-floor heating, frescoed walls, sometimes mosaic floors and usually one large apsed room. There is some evidence for marble panelling. The fine mosaic of the four seasons, displayed on the stairway of the Yorkshire Museum belongs to this period although from another part of the town.

The house at Clementhorpe may have been suburban, separated as it was from the rest of the town by the creek and gully that existed by Skeldergate Bridge and a fourth century burial ground. We do not know, however, the exact boundaries of the *colonia* which was certainly walled. The date and course of its walls are one of the major unsolved problems of York archaeology. Some evidence exists from under the medieval walls opposite the Railway Station, but the only modern evidence relates to the river front where a recent excavation by the York Archaeological Trust in Skeldergate has revealed a defensive wall erected in the fourth century.

Outside the walls of the town were the cemeteries, particularly on The Mount and the site of the railway station. Elaborate tombs and tomb chambers as well as simple graves with little or no markers provided these burial grounds with a varied appearance. One example of a vaulted tomb still survives in the

Tomb relief of a centurion, holding a vine branch, symbol of his rank, in his right hand. Found in Driffield Terrace, The Mount, 1852.

Skeleton of man aged about 40, buried in a wooden coffin in a stone cist. Found Trentholme Drive cemetery, 1952.

cellar of a house on The Mount. In addition amongst the cemeteries and burial gardens were suburban houses or villas such as one at Clementhorpe, with good mosaics, or shops for masons or workers in bone and jet.

The Yorkshire Museum houses a varied collection of finds from the cemeteries which vividly illustrates not only a variety of burial custom but, more important, the everyday life of citizens. In particular the tomb reliefs demonstrate not only the kind of furniture used and clothes worn but also the closeness of family life and the affection lavished on children who often died young. An excavation into a small but crowded cemetery at Trentholme Drive produced 290 skeletons, analysis of which showed not only the cosmopolitan origin of the population and a life expectation much below ours but provided many details of their medical history.

The mixed origins of the people are reflected in the variety of their religious beliefs. The gods worshipped included the classical gods of the Roman pantheon, local Celtic deities, and those of the mystery religions from the east such as Serapis and Mithras. There is also evidence for christianity and as already mentioned York sent its bishop to the council of Arles in A.D. 314.

Trade and Industry

Remains of wharves found along the river Foss included one with the stone base of a tower crane on the site of the Telephone Exchange in Hungate. They belonged to the harbour of a thriving river port that had a direct link by the Ouse and Humber with the sea. The army, which in many things was self-supporting and controlled its own supplies, had its own transports and river pilots, one of whom, M. Minucius Audens of the Sixth legion, dedicated an altar that has survived.   (*See page 26*.)

There were also civilian contractors, and such may have been the wealthy freedman, M. Aurelius Lunaris, who held office in the cities of both Lincoln and York, and in A.D. 237 was shipping direct from York to Bordeaux. The cargo that he took back to York was probably wine, rough stuff for army rations and finer vintages for rich civilian customers. Alternatively he may have carried olive oil for lighting or the kitchen or for use at the baths. Both oil and wine were carried in large jars, which were called *amphorae* because of their two handles. Many fragments of these have been found in York.

Another merchant, called *moritex* or shipper on his coffin, was M. Verecundius Diogenes from Bourges in central France, who with his wife, Julia Fortunata from Sardinia, ended his days a wealthy citizen of York. His inscribed coffin was found in York in the sixteenth century and then travelled as ballast in a river-boat to Hull, where it was last seen in the eighteenth century in use as a horse trough at an inn.

Verecundius like Lunaris was probably engaged in the wine trade. There were other cargoes that might have been brought from Gaul, such as the red glossy tableware known to-day as samian. Other tableware in a fine thin fabric with a dark polished coating and quality glassware were imported from the Rhineland.

Bordeaux was a main port for the British trade and that is why a Rhine-lander like Solimarius Secundinus of Trier, a trader with Britain, settled there. Ships also sailed from the Rhine to Britain. A shrine to the goddess Nehalennia at the mouth of the Rhine received many dedications from traders grateful for the safety of their cargoes. M. Secundinius Silvanus was a merchant in pottery trading with Britain and a member of a rich business family from Trier mainly engaged in the cloth trade.

More interesting for York is L. Viducius Placidus, a citizen of Rouen, whose dedication to Nehalennia was dredged up from the estuary in 1970-1. He described himself as a merchant trading with Britain. In 1976 the York Archaeological Trust recovered from its excavations at Clementhorpe a mutilated and reused stone inscribed with another dedication by the same man, this time to another deity and to the Spirit of the place and the divinities of the emperors. The dedication is dated by the consuls of that year to A.D. 221 and Viducius is again described as a merchant. The two lavish dedications taken together indicate a prosperous commerce between York and the Rhine estuary in the early third century.

Like Secundinius, Viducius probably dealt in pottery and there is room on the damaged part of the stone for the word stating this. The large amount of East Gaulish Samian pottery found at York was probably imported by this route. As a successful merchant with connections outside York, Viducius probably held office like Verecundius and Lunaris as a *sevir*, the magistracy concerned with emperor worship.

The river at York also carried inland traffic. Pennine gritstone was shipped down the Aire and Tadcaster limestone down the Wharfe and thence upstream to York. Barge traffic using the Ouse and Trent and canals such as the Car and Foss Dikes could penetrate far inland and it is probably in this way that the products of the Nene valley kilns reached York, a British tableware that replaced samian in the third century. Other products such as corn, coal, lead and gypsum may have come by road or boat.

York as the military centre for the northern armies was of necessity served by a fine network of roads, and through York must have come not only the rations and military supplies but the luxuries needed both by the soldiers and the civilian communities that had grown up alongside the northern forts, in some cases developing into small towns. York was not only an importing but a distributing centre of some importance.

Roman York also had its manufactures, which were mainly the work of craftsmen who were shopkeepers as well, and who would usually live, work and sell their products in the same long narrow building. The shop end opened onto the street, the workshop was behind and the dwelling upstairs. At Malton a goldsmith's shop was run by a young slave, and many of the York craftsmen were probably of the same status.

Tomb relief of Aelia Aeliana showing her and her husband reclining at a banquet. Found in 1872, N.W. of the station.

Tomb relief of a smith, found in the grounds of the Manor House, Dringhouses, 1860.

A fine tomb relief from York shows a smith wearing a protective leather apron, at work at his anvil with hammer and tongs. A workshop was excavated at Bishophill Senior where in the second century iron was wrought and bronze pins were made. There must have been many such crafts at York although we have direct evidence for only a few, ranging from the stonemasons who carved the fine series of tomb reliefs now in the Yorkshire Museum to carvers and polishers of bone and jet.

Jet is perhaps the most interesting material worked. It comes from near Whitby where it was probably collected from the sea coast rather than mined. The ancients regarded it as possessing magical properties. Some was worked locally into bangles and rings at native settlements in Eskdale, but the quality as well as the Roman design of many of the products implies a more sophisticated centre of manufacture than the native homesteads of N.E. Yorkshire.

Considerable technical skill was needed for making the interlocking and pliable bracelets and necklaces, the well-known portrait pendants, or such pieces as the charming jet leaves from Newton Kyme and the little bear found in Bootham. There is direct evidence for the manufacture of jet objects at York.

The rarity of the material makes the distribution of the product easier to trace. Discoveries such as the pendant, a betrothal gift, recently found at Chesterholm, or the betrothal ring with christian inscription, an older find from Chesters, demonstrate as might be expected a market for York goods in the area of Hadrian's Wall. More remarkable are the many jet articles found in Cologne and now in the Museum there. These were probably made in York and illustrate the two-way flow of York's trade.

Jet bear pendant, found
in Bootham, 1845, with a
coin of Constantine, of
date A.D. 312-5.

Jet oval pendant:
facing busts of
husband and wife.
Place of finding
uncertain.

Clothing was an essential manufacture. Many of the York tomb reliefs illustrate the kind of clothing worn, although perhaps a more formal dress than was worn for everyday. A spindle and whorl found at Bishophill Senior show that hand spinning was done at home. The clothing trade, however, could be lucrative as the tomb at Igel near Trier in Germany of the rich Secundinii family demonstrates.

At York we are lucky that the fourth-century custom of gypsum burial has preserved for us examples of the finely woven linen textiles worn after death. The spindle from Bishophill Senior spun too fine a thread for the wool then available and was probably used for spinning flax. The countryside around York was eminently suitable for growing flax and for the processes involved in preparing the crop, and Roman York was probably a centre for the manufacture of linen cloth.

Altar to Fortune
dedicated by the
wife of a legionary
legate, found on
the site now
occupied by the
Hudson House
railway offices,
in 1839.

Model of Roman burial
vault found in 1807, now
under No. 104 The Mount.

We have no direct evidence that any York textiles were exported abroad. British textiles however were famous in the Roman world and several were included in the list of maximum prices issued by Diocletian. The Secundinii family of Trier derived its wealth from the clothing trade and as we have already mentioned two members of that family were engaged in the British trade, one from Bordeaux and the other exporting pottery direct from the Rhine to Britain. In view of the quality of the York linen cloth and of York's trade connections with the Rhineland it would be surprising if none of this cloth was exported.

Pottery is one industry for which we have evidence of wholesale manufacture in concentrations that suggest organisation on a larger scale than a simple craftsman basis. Fourteen miles north of York, at Crambeck, near Castle Howard, a typical concentration of kilns was excavated by the late Dr. Philip Corder, then a master at Bootham School, York. These kilns were in operation in the late fourth century and their wares had a wide distribution in northern Britain.

'Parisian Ware' beaker: found Trentholme Drive cemetery in 1951.

The Yorkshire Museum

The Yorkshire Museum has very large collections, including most of the material from Roman York. Many of the items referred to in the preceding text are to be found here. Not all of these nor those mentioned below are currently on display at the museum. Newly designed galleries were opened in 1985 to house an excellent exhibition with reconstruction drawings and models which illustrate everyday life in Roman York in an entertaining and informative way.

The inscriptions and tomb reliefs refer to individuals and often name them, providing vivid glimpses of life and society in town and garrison. One of the commanding officers, Hieronymianus, and his temple to Serapis have already been mentioned, but there is also another, Antonius Isauricus, whose wife, Sosia Iuncina, dedicated an alter to Fortune which she had placed in the large bath-house in the *colonia*.

The centurions are represented by a fine coffin with a pair of cupids flanking the inscription panel. (*See above*.) Septimius Lupianus buried in it his wife, Julia Victorina, and his infant son Constantius. The standard-bearer L. Duccius Rufinus died at the age of 28. Born in Vienne in Gaul, he came to York to serve in the Ninth Legion, and, carved in stone, still stands holding a standard in his right hand. Other soldiers and veterans have their memorials including the little altar set up by a legionary pilot, but none seems so sad as the beautifully carved coffin that the centurion Felicius Simplex bought for his little daughter, Simplicia Florentina, 'most innocent soul'. (*See below*.)

Tombstone of Duccius Rufinus (See page 25).

Altar dedicated by M. Minucius Audens, soldier and pilot of the Sixth Legion to the Mother Goddesses of Africa, Italy and Gaul (See page 20).

Among the smaller relics of the garrison are two bronze camp kettles, each inscribed with the name of the century that owned it. Life in the army is illustrated by other items such as a helmet dredged out of the Tyne, and fragments of military equipment found in Yorkshire.

Among the civilians there is the coffin of Aelia Severa, wife or daughter of a decurion who was a member of the governing body of a town. Her husband had been Caecilius Rufus whose freedman and heir, Caecilius Musicus, had arranged for her burial. Flavius Bellator was another decurion who died at the age of 29.

Julia Fortunata whose husband was the *sevir* Verecundius Diogenes came from Sardinia. A *sevir augustalis* was one of the magistrates concerned with the cult of the emperor's divinity which was the symbol of the loyalty of each community. This group of six colleagues, hence the name, was attractive to the wealthy freedmen merchants, who because they were not free-born were unable to hold any of the other offices in the *colonia*.

Tomb reliefs showing husband and wife, and funeral banquet scenes give glimpses of everyday life, but these can be found more vividly among the small ordinary objects, pins and brooches, a fan handle, the frame of a parasol,

Charioteer's or gladiator's
lucky charm.

Stamp used on ointment by an
oculist. Now at Gray's Court.

lamps, keys, spoons and combs, and case on case of serried rows of Roman crockery. A christian motto in bone, 'Welcome sister, may you live long in god', originally adorned the trinket box in which a Roman lady kept her mirror and her beads and bangles, all buried with her when she died. A little bone plaque inscribed, 'Lord Victor, good luck and victory', was found on a skeleton and was the kind of lucky charm worn by a gladiator or a charioteer.

The most important collection outside the Yorkshire Museum is that at Gray's Court. From it the small object illustrated (above right) is a stamp that was used by the oculist, Julius Alexander, to mark a cake of ointment for sore eyes. Outside York at Malton, the Malton Museum has an interesting collection of Roman material that is in many respects complementary to that in the Yorkshire Museum.

Head of the
Emperor
Constantine the
Great. Found in
Stonegate.

Recent Excavations in Roman York

The York Archaeological Trust was formed in 1972 to carry out rescue excavations and research in the City of York. The results of some of its work have been incorporated in the preceding pages. Under the vigorous direction of Peter Addyman it has added much to our knowledge of all periods of the city's life and has added to the Roman monuments by exposing for permanent exhibition the sewer in Church Street illustrated below.

Legionary Fortress: View along Roman Sewer under buildings adjacent to Swinegate, discovered 1972.